FRETLESS BASS

by Bunny Brunel & Josquin des Prés

PLAYBACK+
Speed • Pitch • Balance • Loop

To access audio visit:
www.halleonard.com/mylibrary

Enter Code
2922-5044-6323-3777

ISBN 978-0-634-04578-3

HAL•LEONARD®
7777 W. BLUEMOUND RD. P.O. BOX 13819 MILWAUKEE, WI 53213

In Australia Contact:
Hal Leonard Australia Pty. Ltd.
4 Lentara Court
Cheltenham, Victoria, 3192 Australia
Email: ausadmin@halleonard.com.au

Visit Hal Leonard Online at
www.halleonard.com

Contents

CHAPTER 1 • Fretless Bass Fundamentals

CHAPTER 2 • Various Techniques

CHAPTER 3 • Styles

CHAPTER 4 • Performance

Recording Credits

Bunny Brunel and Josquin des Prés, fretless bass (on all Tracks)
Dede Ceccarelli, drums (Tracks 62 to 69)
Bernie Torelli, guitar (Track 63)
Phil Higgins, guitar (Tracks 42 to 61)
Edited and Mastered at Track Star Studios by Tristan des Prés

"Listen Now" (Track 33)
Bunny Brunel, fretless bass
Dede Ceccarelli, drums
Daniel Goyone, piano
Jean Pierre Massiera, engineer
Mixed by Bunny Brunel

"As My Brother" (Track 70)
Bunny Brunel, fretless bass
Bernie Torelli, guitar
Daniel Goyone, keyboards
Jean Paul Ceccarelli, drums
Joe Farrell, tenor sax
Bill Watrous, trombone
Al Vizutti, trumpet
Jean Pierre Massiera, engineer
Mixed by Bernie Torelli

"First Flight" (Track 71)
Josquin des Prés, fretless bass (solo lines)
Steve Mitchell, fretless bass (rhythm lines)
Tristan des Prés, keyboards
Jerry Goodman, violin
Bob Campbell, sax
Calvin Lakin, drums
Mike Harris, engineer
Mixed by Josquin des Prés

Acknowledgments

Special thanks to Carvin for the Bunny Brunel BB75 and BB70 Basses and Amps, Mackie for the amazing d8b digital board, Labella for the great strings, Hipshot for the bass extender key, and Art for the DI/O preamp. Thanks to MOTU for recording software and hardware, Monster Cable Products, Audio Geer, Tannoy for the great 800A monitor system, and Nomad Factory digital audio plug-ins. Thanks also to everyone at Hal Leonard Corporation, Emmy Brunel, Lisa Vu, The Keisel brothers, Dave Flores, Richard Cruz, Greg Mackie, DK Sweet, Dan Moore, Richard Cocco, Bob Archigian, David Borisoff, Phil Betette, Thad Wharton, Irv Weisman, John Borja, Jim Cooper, Bernie Torelli, and Tristan Des Prés.

Cover photos by Richard Cruz

Inside photos by Emmy Brunel

Introduction

Grammy nominee and fretless bass pioneer Bunny Brunel teams up with best-selling author and session bass player Josquin des Prés to offer the first book/audio tutorial dedicated solely to the development of skills on the fretless bass.

Fretless Bass covers all aspects of the instrument since its appearance in popular music in the early seventies. From intonation exercises to glissandos, from vibrato to the use of Bunny's signature invention, sliding harmonics, *Fretless Bass* approaches teaching the instrument through a wide array of exercises, melodies, grooves, and solos performed by two world-renowned bassists.

Bunny Brunel

When Chick Corea watched Bernard Bunny Brunel play one night at an upscale London jazz club in 1978, Bunny was unaware of the ultimate significance Corea would play in his future success as a bassist. A few weeks after that visit to London, Chick called Bunny and asked him to pack up and join him on a worldwide tour. Bunny quickly accepted and went on to record the classics "Tap Step" and "Secret Agent" with the legendary jazz fusionist. The roster of artists Bunny went on to record and perform with is practically a "who's who" of music industry giants. Notables include Herbie Hancock, Wayne Shorter, Tony Williams, Al Jarreau, Natalie Cole, Larry Coryell, Al Dimeola, Mike Stern, Joe Farrell, and a list that goes on and on.

Besides his work as a performer, he is equally at home in the roles of composer, arranger, and producer. As a soundtrack composer, Bunny collaborated with Clint Eastwood in creating the main theme ("Claudia's Theme") for the Oscar winning film, *The Unforgiven.* He also worked on several TV shows, including the popular series *Highlander.*

As a designer, Bunny created a line of electric bass guitars for Carvin and an electric upright bass. Bunny has released many albums, including *Momentum, Ivanhoe, Touch, Dedication, For You to Play, L.A. Zoo,* and *Cab.* His latest album, *Cab 2,* has been nominated for the Best Contemporary Jazz Instrumental Album Grammy award of 2002. These projects highlight his beautiful compositions and melodic solos and show off his breathtaking bass lines.

Taking an active interest in helping bass players, Brunel regularly gives seminars and lessons on his unique approach to the instrument. He has written several books and instructional videos.

Josquin des Prés

Session bass player, author, producer, and songwriter Josquin des Prés began his career in France in the mid seventies when he obtained his first record deal, signing his fusion band with United Artists Records. He's since worked on hundreds of projects along side some of the biggest names in the music industry. Shared credits include studio notables such as Jeff Porcaro, Alex Acuna, Vinny Colaiuta, Jerry Donahue, Billy Sheehan, Jimmy Crespo, Jerry Goodman, Steve Lukather, Didier Lockwood, David Garibaldi, and many others.

In addition to his career as a bass player Josquin has authored fourteen best-selling bass instruction books, two guitar instruction books, and released *Old School Funk Bass,* distributed by Big Fish Audio, a CD-ROM of over 500 of his funkiest bass lines in audio and Acid Loop formats.

Josquin has also taken an interest in matters pertaining to the music industry and the success of musicians within the business. This has lead to the writing of two self-help titles: *Creative Careers in Music* and *Reality Check.*

As a producer and songwriter, Josquin has worked on hundreds of recordings and has had numerous songs covered by international artists. He is one of the very few to collaborate on several songs with Elton John's legendary lyricist Bernie Taupin.

Chapter One

Fretless Bass Fundamentals

Hand Position

On the fretless bass, proper hand and finger position is crucial in producing the right note. On a fretted instrument, you can place your finger anywhere between two frets. The fret itself determines the pitch.

Hand position on fretted bass:

On a fretless bass, you will need to place your finger slightly behind the fret mark of the desired note in order to attain accurate intonation.

Hand position on fretless bass:

Fingering and Intonation Exercise

Here we'll use one finger per fret ascending over four strings and descending over five strings.

Pay close attention to your thumb and finger positioning in this exercise. Play each note precisely and distinctively.

TRACK 1

Scale Exercise in C Major

We ascend through the C major scale here over four strings and descend over five strings.

TRACK 2

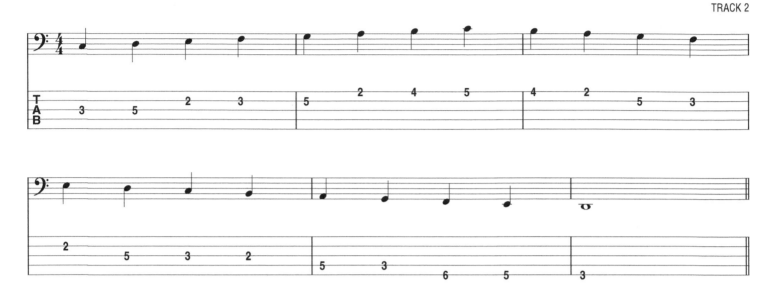

Interval Exercises in C Major

In this section, we're going to be concentrating on the intervals of the C major scale. Each example will ascend through three strings and descend through five.

3rds

TRACK 3

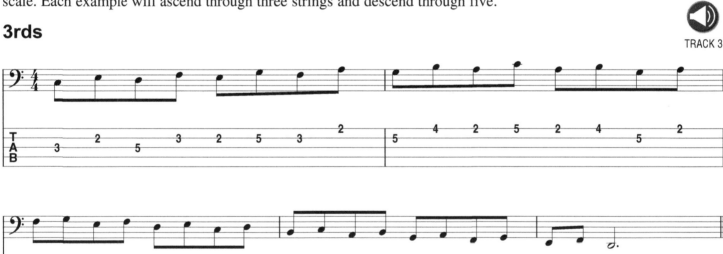

4ths

TRACK 4

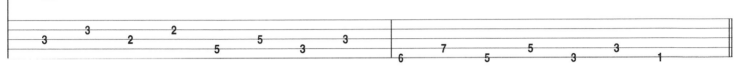

5ths

TRACK 5

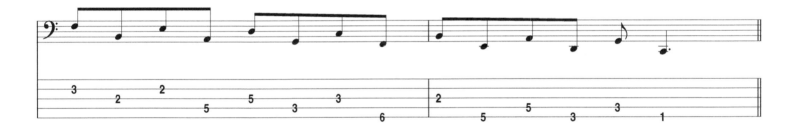

6ths

TRACK 6

Pattern Exercises in C Major

Here we're going to be learning longer patterns in the C major scale that will continue to work on intonation.

In this exercise, we're ascending in ascending groups of four over three strings and descending in descending groups of four over five strings.

TRACK 7

As a variation, here we're ascending with descending groups of four and descending with ascending groups of four.

TRACK 8

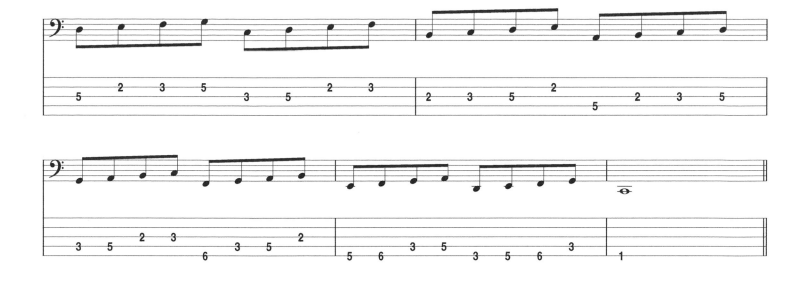

Now we'll combine the two above ideas. We'll ascend in an ascending/descending eight-note pattern and descend in an ascending/descending eight-note pattern.

TRACK 9

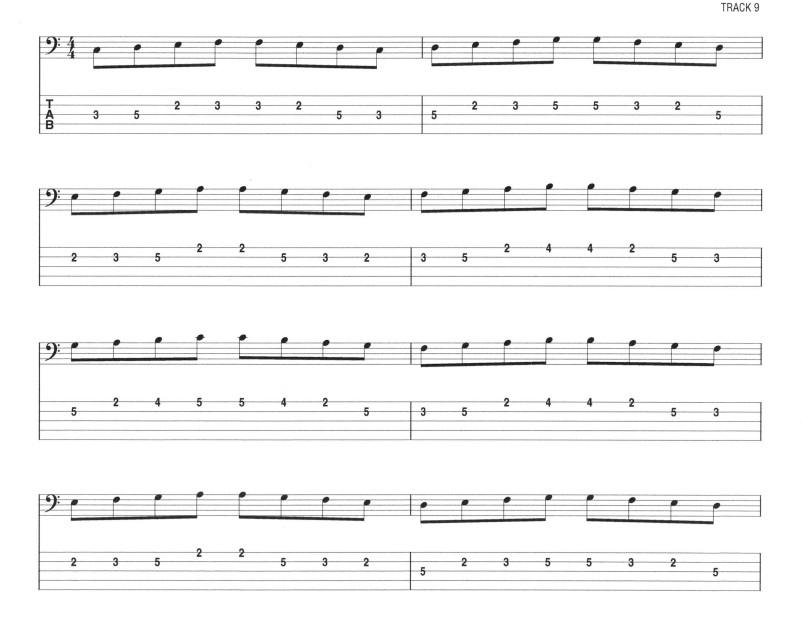

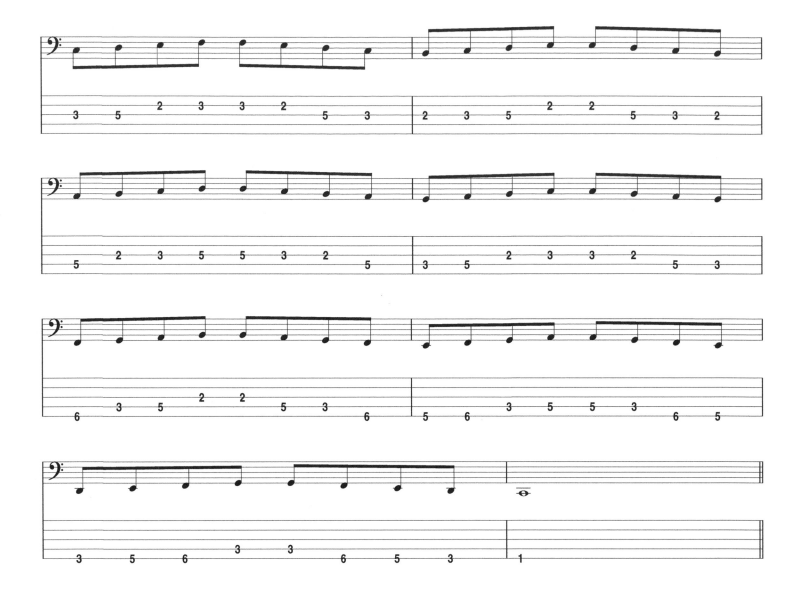

Modal Exercises

Here we'll play through all of the modes in C. Each one will ascend over three strings and descend over five strings.

C IONIAN

TRACK 10

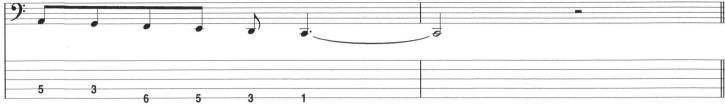

D DORIAN

E PHRYGIAN

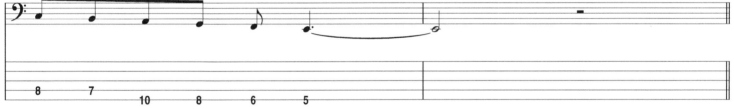

F LYDIAN

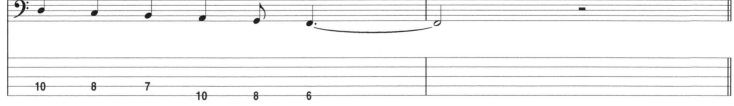

G MIXOLYDIAN

TRACK 14

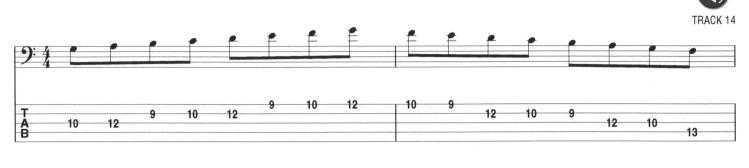

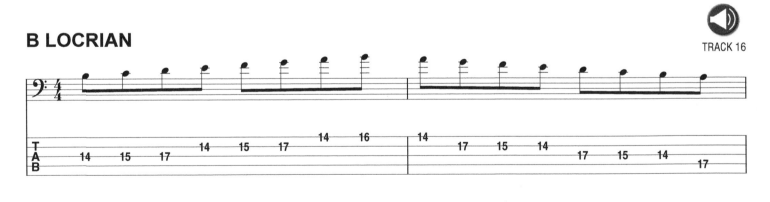

A AEOLIAN

TRACK 15

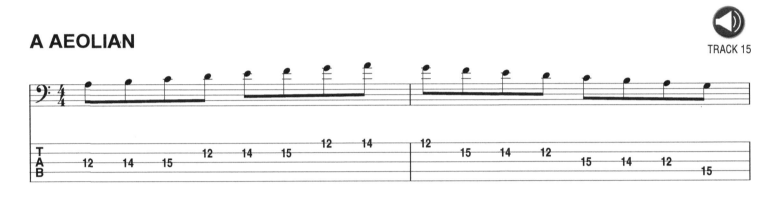

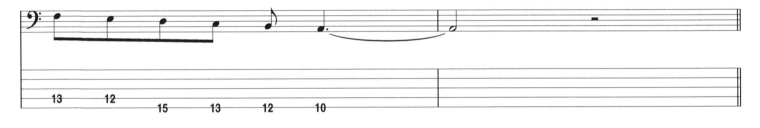

B LOCRIAN

TRACK 16

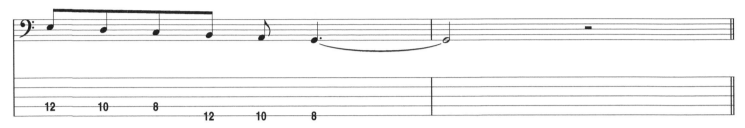

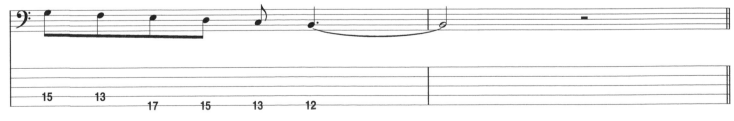

Chapter Two
Various Techniques

Vibrato

Here we'll concentrate on playing some grooves that make use of vibrato. When applying vibrato, it's best to wait until the end of the note. Attack the note first and then add slight vibrato.

TRACK 17

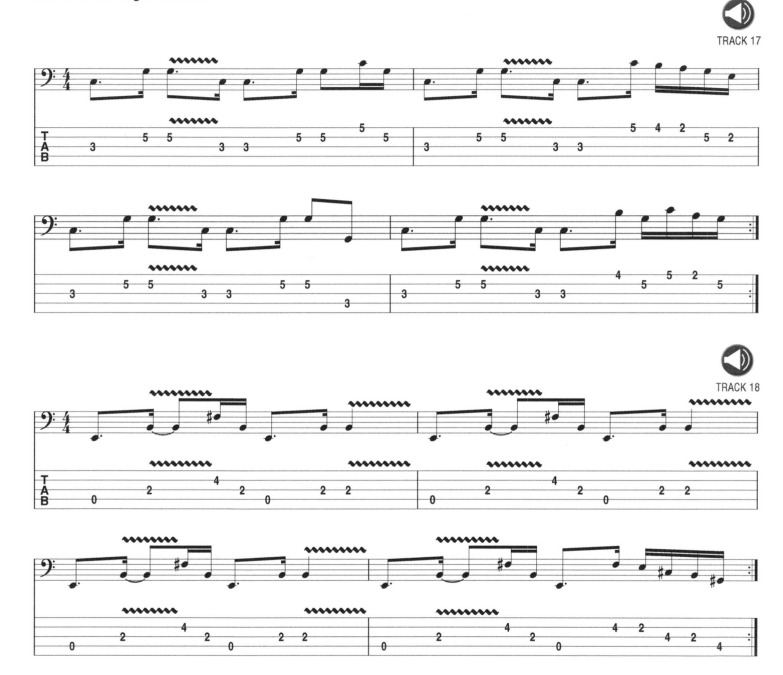

TRACK 18

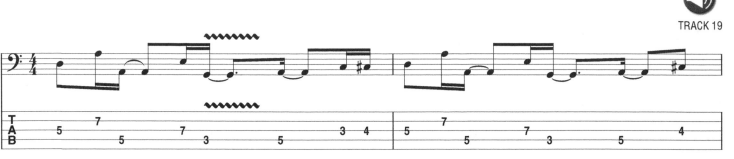

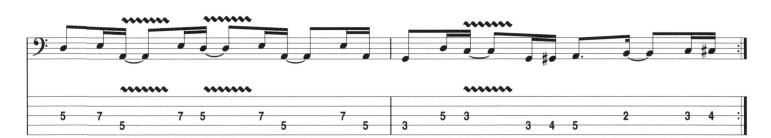

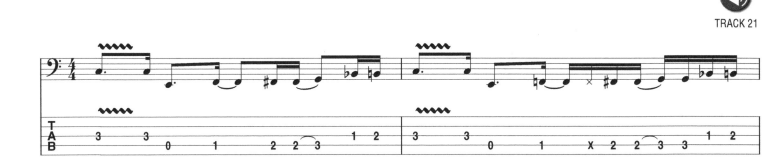

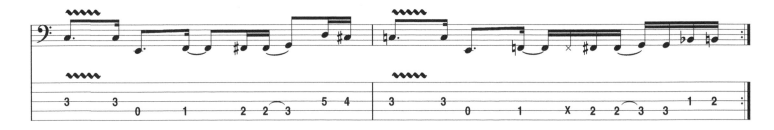

TRACK 22

TRACK 23

TRACK 24

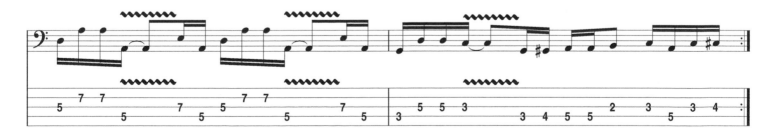

Slides

When using slides on the fretless bass, the timing is crucial. You must slightly anticipate the slide in order to reach the destination note at the desired beat. Therefore, pay close attention to the rhythm in these examples. Your slides need to be rhythmically accurate.

TRACK 25

TRACK 26

TRACK 27

Combining Vibrato and Slides with Octaves

In this section, we're going to be playing grooves that make use of vibrato, slides, and octaves. Try playing the grooves sustaining the octaves at first. This will help to ensure proper intonation.

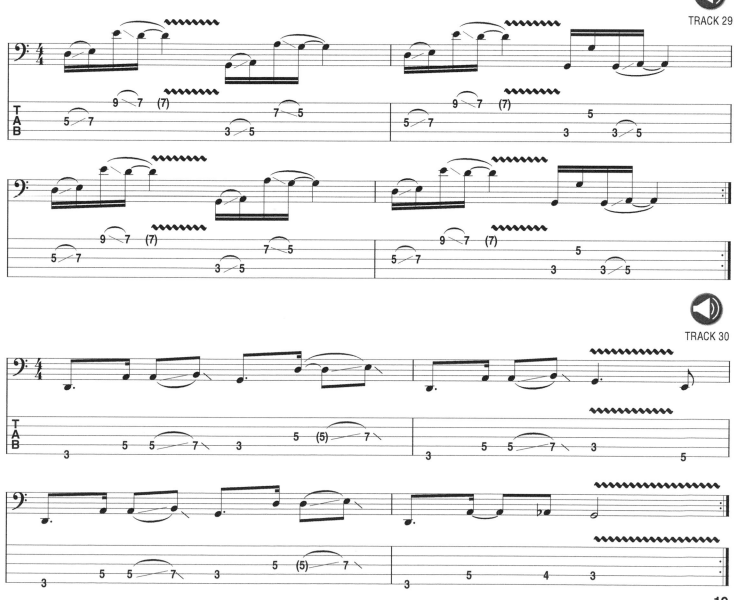

Melody Lines

When playing melodies on the fretless bass, the best advice we can give is to approach the instrument as if it were the human voice. Practice playing melodies that you know well and don't hesitate to overemphasize and emulate all the inflections of a human voice. Focus on dynamics, feel, and interpretation. The chances of sounding "corny" on the fretless bass are very slim, so feel free to use vibrato and glissando (slide) techniques as much as you'd like.

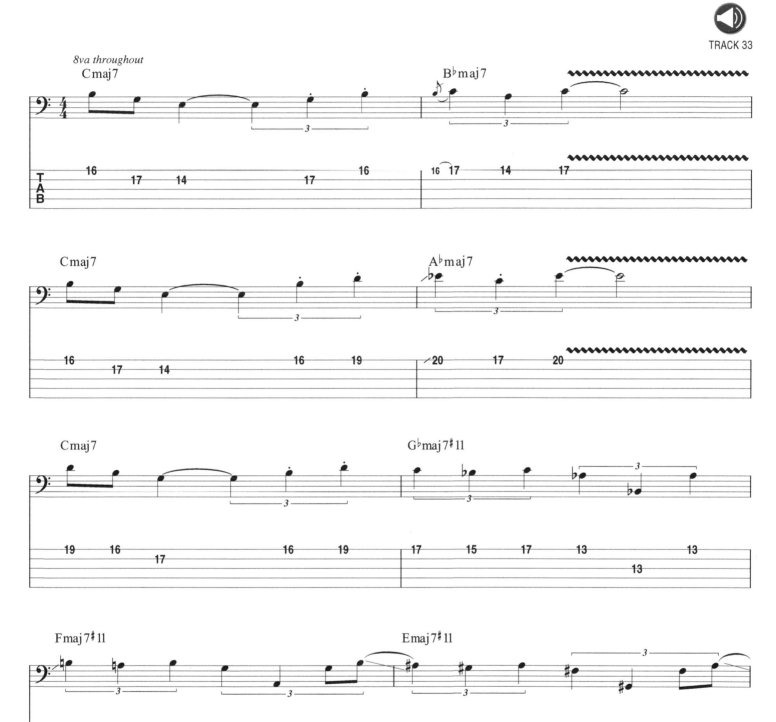

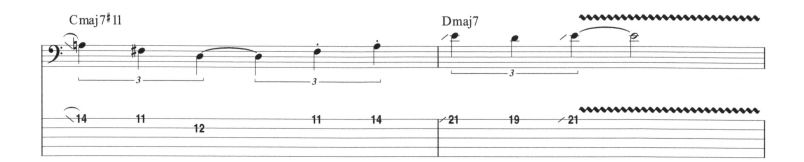

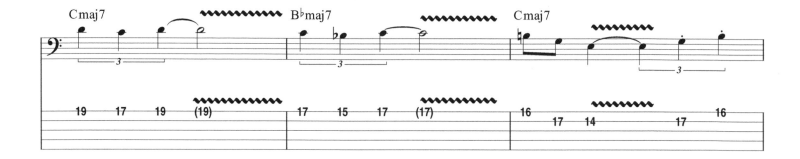

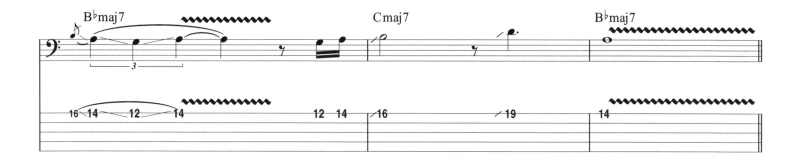

Double Stops

When playing double stops on the fretless bass, it's important to pay attention to intonation on both notes. This is especially true when using two fingers to play a perfect 4th.

TRACK 34

TRACK 35

2nd time only

TRACK 36

TRACK 37

Sliding Harmonics

In order to execute a sliding harmonic, first strike a harmonic and then quickly push the string against the fingerboard and slide to the desired note. This technique allows you to maintain the sound of a natural harmonic on notes other than those related to the open-string harmonic series.

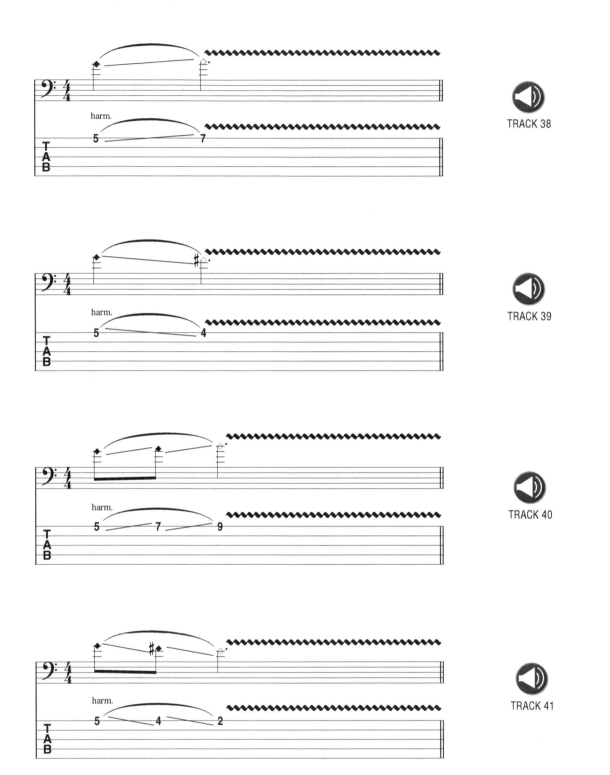

TRACK 38

TRACK 39

TRACK 40

TRACK 41

Chapter Three

Styles

In this section, we're going to be playing through grooves in various styles. Refer to the full backing tracks so you can hear the roll of the bass within the rhythm section.

POP

There are many shades of pop music, and here we'll look at a few different sub-styles that pop is commonly divided in to. Pay attention to the role that each instrument fills—not just the bass.

Pop Ballad

TRACK 42

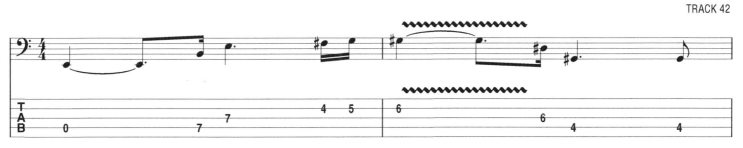

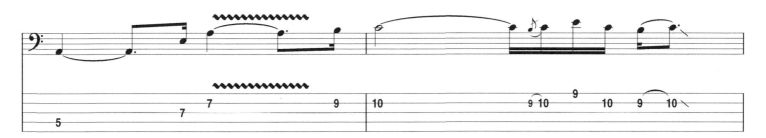

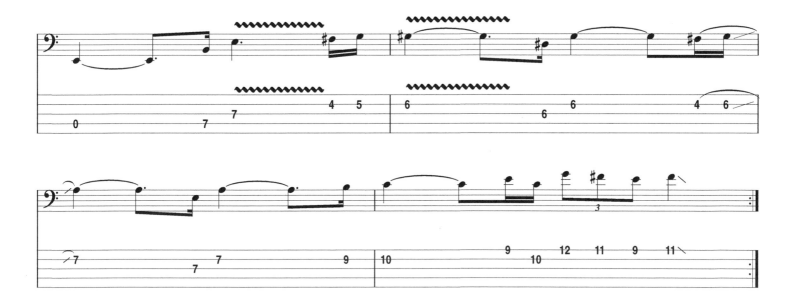

Pop Ballad

Pop Medium Tempo

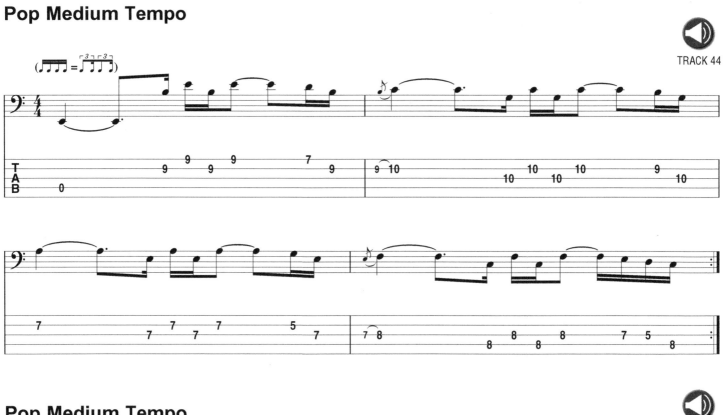

Pop Medium Tempo

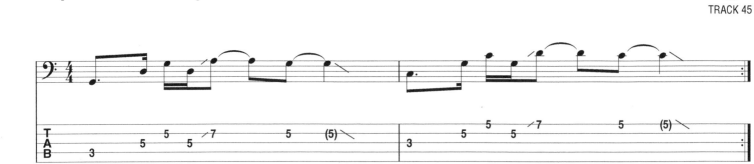

Pop Ballad

TRACK 46

Pop Ballad

TRACK 47

Pop Medium Tempo

TRACK 48

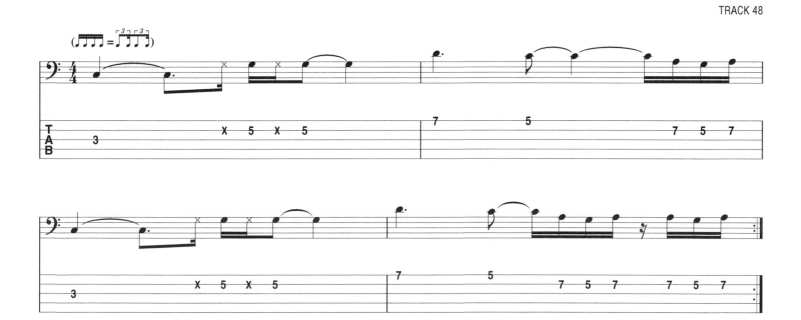

Pop Medium Tempo

TRACK 49

Pop Medium Tempo

TRACK 50

Pop Medium Tempo

TRACK 51

Pop Medium Tempo

TRACK 52

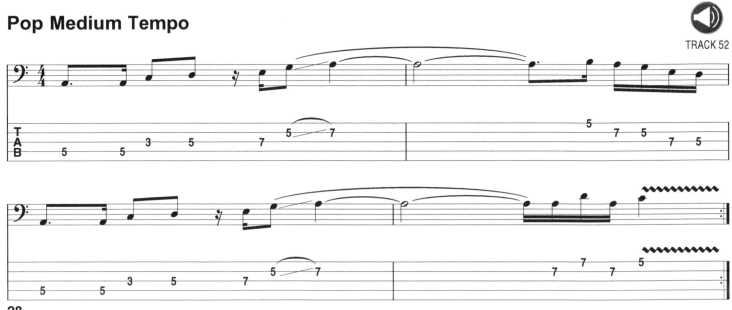

Pop Medium Tempo

Pop Medium Tempo

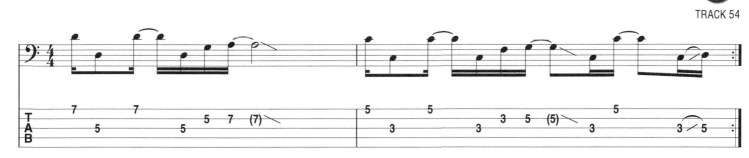

Pop Medium Tempo

FUNK

Here we find an example of low-down grooving funk. Make sure you're really in the pocket with this one. The power of this music lies almost solely in the groove.

LATIN

In these examples, we'll explore a few Latin styles. As with the funk example, rhythm plays a big role in these lines.

Latin Pop

TRACK 57

Latin Pop

TRACK 58

Latin Pop

TRACK 59

Traditional Latin

TRACK 60

Traditional Latin

TRACK 61

FUSION

Here we'll take a look at some various fusion examples. It is recommended that you practice the first two examples slowly until you get the lines securely under your fingers. Once you're comfortable with them you can begin to aim for the tempo on the tracks.

Funk Fusion

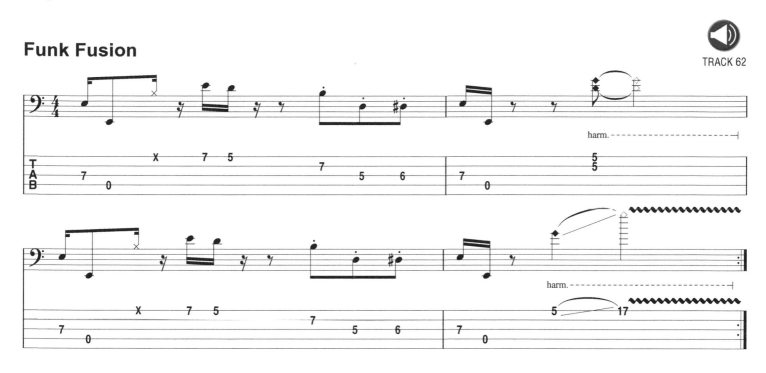

TRACK 62

Funk Fusion

TRACK 63

Funk Fusion

TRACK 64

Funk Fusion

TRACK 65

Latin Jazz Fusion

TRACK 66

Latin Jazz Fusion

TRACK 67

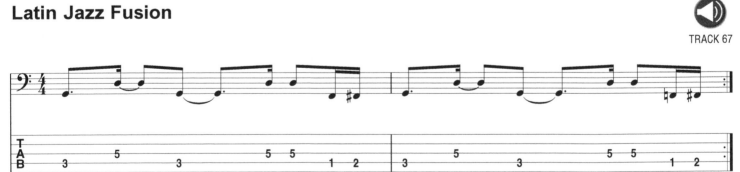

Latin Jazz Fusion

Latin Jazz Fusion

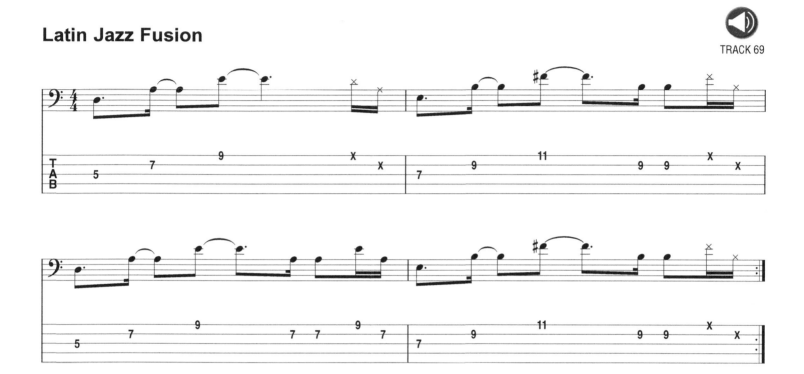

Chapter Four

Performance

"As My Brother"

(Bunny Brunel)

TRACK 70

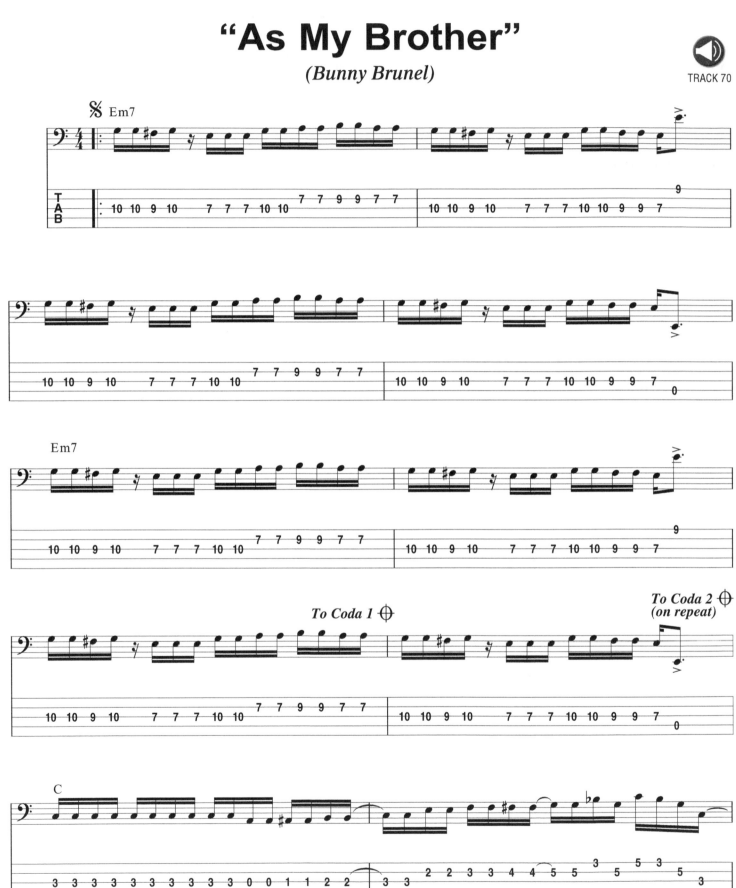

C

D.S. al Coda 1

⊕ *Coda 1*

Em7   D13sus4

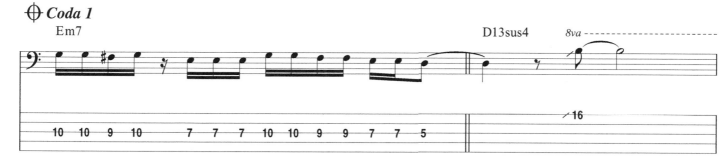

Cm/D

D13sus4

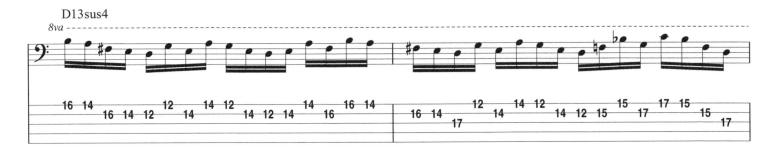

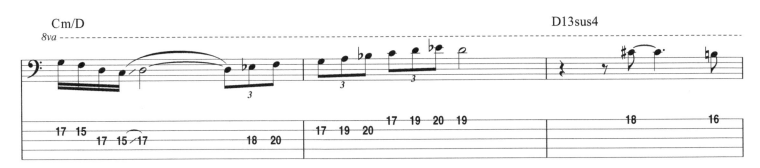

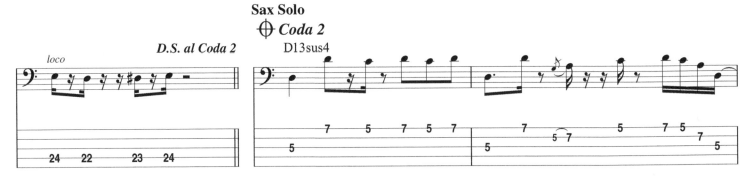

Sax Solo

"First Flight"
(Tristan des Prés)

Tune down 1/2 step:
(low to high) E♭–A♭–D♭–G♭

Intro

Verse

Bass 2 tacet
Bass 1

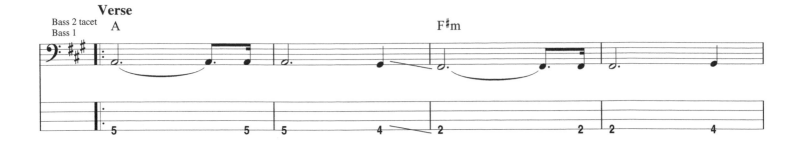

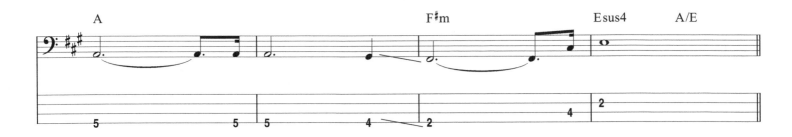

Bridge

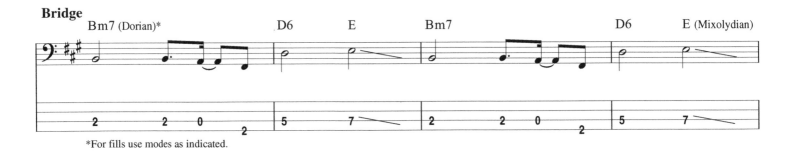

*For fills use modes as indicated.

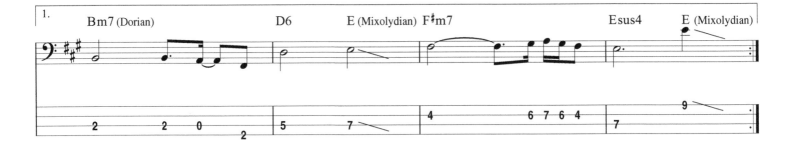

Sax Solo

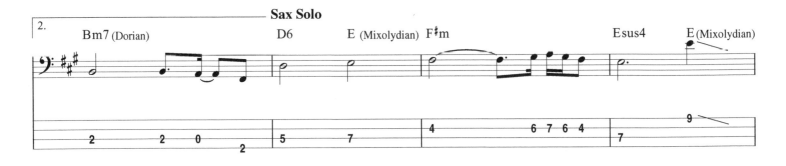

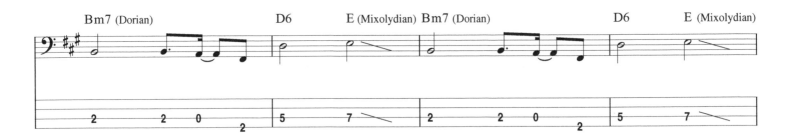

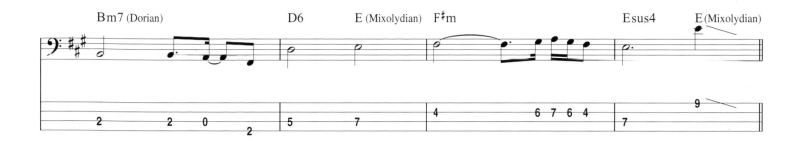

Interlude

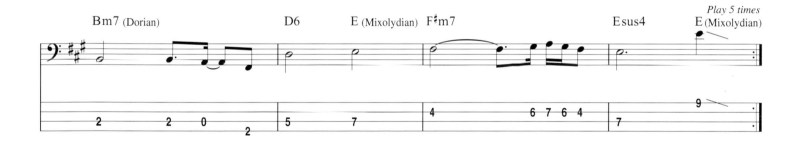

Violin Solo

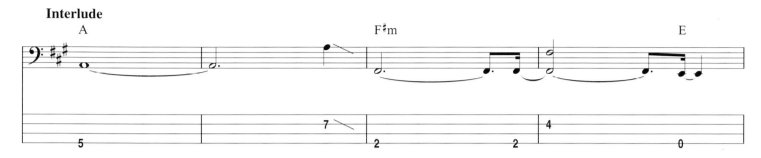

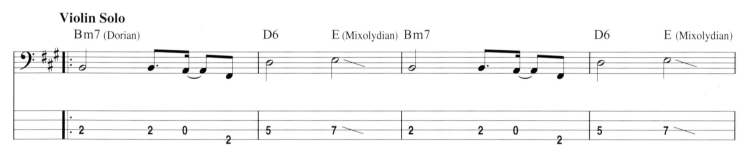

Outro

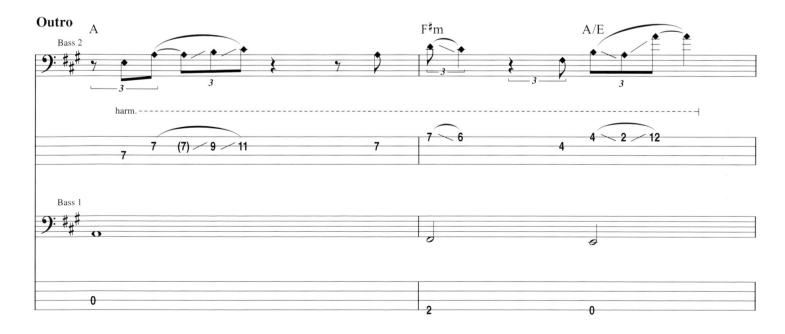

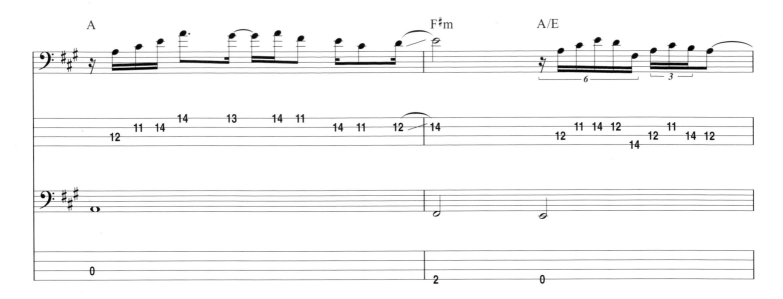

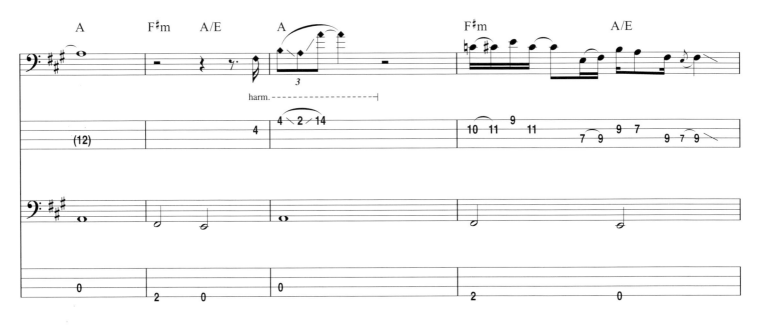

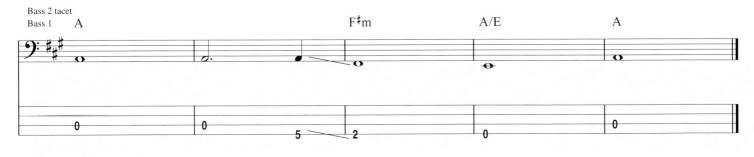